Media Literacy for Kids

Learning About
Privacy

by Martha E. H. Rustad

Consulting Editor: Gail Saunders-Smith, PhD

Consultant: JoAnne DeLurey Reed
Librarian and Teacher, Scroggins Elementary School
Houston, Texas

CAPSTONE PRESS
a capstone imprint

Pebble Plus is published by Capstone Press,
1710 Roe Crest Drive, North Mankato, Minnesota 56003
www.capstonepub.com

Library of Congress Cataloging-in-Publication Data
Rustad, Martha E. H. (Martha Elizabeth Hillman), 1975–
 Learning about privacy / by Martha E. H. Rustad.
   pages cm.—(Pebble plus. Media literacy for kids)
 Includes bibliographical references and index.
  ISBN 978-1-4914-1832-1 (library binding)—ISBN 978-1-4914-1837-6 (ebook pdf)
 1. Internet and children—Safety measures—Juvenile literature. 2. Privacy, Right of—
Juvenile literature. I. Title.
 HQ784.I58R87 2015
 323.44'8—dc23   2014023675

Editorial Credits
Erika L. Shores, editor; Sarah Bennett, designer; Gene Bentdahl, production specialist

Photo Credits
All photos Capstone Studio: Karon Dubke except: Capstone Press, 11, (inset website), 13;
Shutterstock: M.Stasy, cover, 11, 13, Peter Bernik, 7 (top left), Redshinestudio, 11 (inset
login), Rocketclips, Inc. (top right), 7, Sergey Nivens, cover (background)

Note to Parents and Teachers

The Media Literacy for Kids set supports Common Core State
Standards related to language arts. This book describes and illustrates
the importance of privacy online. The images support early readers in
understanding the text. The repetition of words and phrases helps early
readers learn new words. This book also introduces early readers to
subject-specific vocabulary words, which are defined in the Glossary
section. Early readers may need assistance to read some words and to
use the Table of Contents, Glossary, Read More, Internet Sites, Critical
Thinking Using the Common Core, and Index sections of the book.

Printed in the United States of America in Stevens Point, Wisconsin.
092014   008479WZS15

Table of Contents

Privacy Please!

Privacy means keeping something to oneself. Only trust close friends and family with some ideas. Don't tell strangers private information.

The Internet is full of strangers.

Everyone can see what

is online.

Tell a parent if a website asks for information about you. Some people try to steal information. They might even pretend to be you.

Keep It to Yourself

Learn what information

to keep secret. Never use

your real name on a website.

Your age and email address

should be private too.

Staying private means

not letting strangers find you.

While online do not give out

your phone number or address.

Sign up for newsletter ⊗

Email

Name

Phone Number

☐ Yes!   No Thanks

Why are fish so smart?

[click to see answer]

JOKE of the DAY

Don't say where you go to school. Keep your plans for after school to yourself.

Usernames and Passwords

Some websites ask for a username.
A safe username keeps you
private. A username should not
be your real name. Include
a number in your username.

My Websites
* email   username
           mustang5dA

* myon.com   username
              starreader 123

A password is like a lock.
Passwords should be hard
to guess. Use letters, numbers,
and symbols. Don't tell friends
your passwords.

My Websites

* email   username   mustang529
            passwords   applecat222?

* mnlpn.com username   starreader123
             15books26*

Sharing ideas online can be fun.

Be aware of who can see

your private information.

Be smart and be safe online.

Activity: Make a Strong Password

A strong password must be hard to guess. Use these tips to come up with a good password.

What You Need
paper
pencil

1. Write down your favorite animal. Do you like snakes? Tigers or wolves?

2. Think of a silly way to describe the animal, such as a slow cheetah or a funny turtle. It can be anything, as long as you can remember it.

3. Write down your favorite number. It could be your cousin's birthday or your friend's age. Or how many pets you have.

4. Put the words and numbers together. Add some capital letters and symbols. A few examples might be:

Pink&Panda11 $tinkyKitty42

5. Memorize your password. Share it only with your parents so they can help you if you forget it.

1fi$h2FISH

57FuzzyCat75

2blueDOGz

Glossary

online—to be connected to the Internet

password—a secret word or phrase that lets you in

private—something that is secret or for only one person

stranger—a person you do not know

symbol—something that stands for something else

username—a group of letters or numbers that let you in to a website

website—a place people can go on the Internet

Read More

Gaines, Ann Graham. *Master the Library and Media Center*. Ace It! Information Literacy Series. Berkeley Heights, N.J.: Enslow Publishers, 2009.

Grayson, Robert. *Managing Your Digital Footprint*. Digital and Information Literacy. New York: Rosen Central, 2011.

Jakubiak, David J. *A Smart Kid's Guide to Internet Privacy*. Kids Online. New York: PowerKids Press, 2010.

Internet Sites

FactHound offers a safe, fun way to find Internet sites related to this book. All of the sites on FactHound have been researched by our staff.

Here's all you do:

Visit *www.facthound.com*

Type in this code: 9781491418321

Super-cool stuff! Check out projects, games and lots more at www.capstonekids.com

Critical Thinking Using the Common Core

Name two ways to stay private online.
(Key Ideas and Details)

Describe how to create a safe username.
(Key Ideas and Details)

Index

Word Count: 183
Grade: 1
Early-Intervention Level: 21